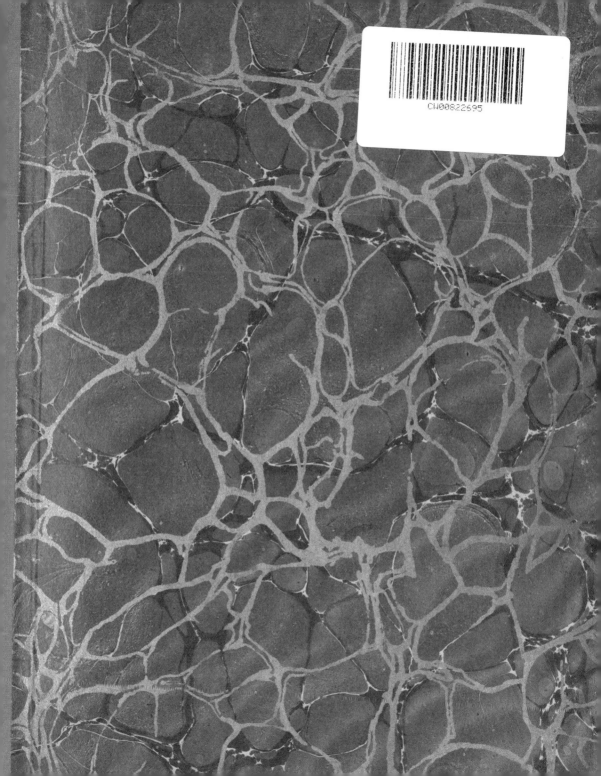

Dear Alison

A New Zealand Soldier's story from Stalag 383

Edited by
Simon Pollard

Dedicated to Dudley Roberts Muff

PENGUIN BOOKS
Published by the Penguin Group
Penguin Group (NZ), 67 Apollo Drive, Rosedale,
North Shore 0632, New Zealand (a division of Pearson New Zealand Ltd)
Penguin Group (USA) Inc., 375 Hudson Street,
New York, New York 10014, USA
Penguin Group (Canada), 90 Eglinton Avenue East, Suite 700, Toronto,
Ontario, M4P 2Y3, Canada (a division of Pearson Penguin Canada Inc.)
Penguin Books Ltd, 80 Strand, London, WC2R 0RL, England
Penguin Ireland, 25 St Stephen's Green,
Dublin 2, Ireland (a division of Penguin Books Ltd)
Penguin Group (Australia), 250 Camberwell Road, Camberwell,
Victoria 3124, Australia (a division of Pearson Australia Group Pty Ltd)
Penguin Books India Pvt Ltd, 11, Community Centre,
Panchsheel Park, New Delhi – 110 017, India
Penguin Books (South Africa) (Pty) Ltd, 24 Sturdee Avenue,
Rosebank, Johannesburg 2196, South Africa

Penguin Books Ltd, Registered Offices: 80 Strand, London, WC2R 0RL, England

First published by Penguin Group (NZ), 2009
10 9 8 7 6 5 4 3 2 1

Copyright © Simon Pollard, 2009

The right of Simon Pollard to be identified as the author of this work in terms of
section 96 of the Copyright Act 1994 is hereby asserted.

Designed by Cheryl Rowe
Prepress by Image Centre Ltd
Printed by Everbest Printing Co. Ltd, China

ISBN 978 0 14330460 9

A catalogue record for this book is available
from the National Library of New Zealand.

www.penguin.co.nz

'Let us not burden our remembrance with,
A heaviness that has gone'

The Tempest

Dudley Roberts Muff's life fitted rather neatly into the twentieth century. He was born in Christchurch, New Zealand on 16 February, when the new century was just six weeks old. He died in Christchurch on 2 January 1995, six weeks before his 95th birthday and almost fifty years after the end of World War Two. Unquestionably, his legacy is the diary he wrote while a prisoner of war in Germany during one of the most tumultuous events of the last century.

The chain of events that led to his capture started when, as part of the 20th Battalion of the 4th Brigade of the 2nd New Zealand Expeditionary Force, he was transferred from Egypt to Greece in early March 1941.

Along with over 16 000 other New Zealanders, he was part of a 60 000 strong British and Commonwealth force defending Greece against a German invasion that was moving south from Yugoslavia and Bulgaria. Towards the end of April, a massive evacuation was organised to stop the retreating allies from being overwhelmed by the Germans. 4th Brigade, along with other New Zealand and Australian forces, was in a rearguard position west of Athens to slow the German advance. This allowed approximately 50 000 soldiers to be evacuated from the southern beaches by ship over a number of nights and taken to Crete. 4th Brigade was meant to travel south on 26 April and be evacuated that night. However, about 1500 German paratroopers who had landed early in the morning blocked their southern retreat across the Corinth Canal and Dudley was captured. As he wrote six months later to his brother Will, *'On April 26 I lay among some Olive Trees about 3 ft. high and was assailed by bomb and machine gun fire from 6 am to 8 am and didn't dare move. At 8.30 p.m. I was a P.O.W.'*

A common phrase used by German soldiers when they captured allied prisoners was, 'For you the war is over,' while the allies themselves often referred to it as 'going into the bag'. On the back

German portrait of New Zealand prisoners of war at Spittal Camp. Dudley is in the third row from the front and is the third man sitting from the left.

page of his soldier's book, Dudley just wrote, *'Captured April 26th 41 Sat. at approx 8'.*

Within a few days, 1850 New Zealanders had become prisoners of war in Greece, including 80 men from the 20th Battalion. Remarkably, all but four of these eighty men survived being held in Germany over the next four years. A few weeks later the equally disastrous campaign in Crete would result in another 2200 New Zealanders becoming prisoners of war, the largest number captured in one battle in New Zealand's military history.

Dudley and most of the other allied prisoners were marched to a transit camp in Corinth, Greece. If the days before his capture had seemed like hell on earth with his battalion under constant attack from German aircraft, the camp must

have seemed like Dante's inferno where many who entered abandoned all hope. Almost 5000 men were herded into a holding pen in a sandy area on the outskirts of the city. There was little shelter from the sun and blistering heat and it took hours of queuing for everybody to get their daily allowance of just over a litre of water from a single well. The only food provided each day was something resembling a dog biscuit and a watery soup that, on a good day, had been enriched with the meat from a single donkey for the whole camp. Any buildings were virtually uninhabitable because of flies and bedbugs. The toilet facilities added to the wretched conditions, as they only had an 'open-trench latrine' almost 200-metres long.

Sickness spread rapidly through the camp

and less than a week into his incarceration Dudley suffered from dysentery and dehydration. He was admitted to a make-shift hospital in a hotel in Corinth and then to the nearby prisoner of war hospital in Kokkinia. Here, an officer gathered next-of-kin details from the New Zealand patients. Dudley gave his sister Win as his contact, saying that she lived at Chester Street, Christchurch, but he couldn't remember the street number. In what turned out to be a remarkable coincidence, someone else in the group called out '87'. It was Win's postman from Christchurch and luckily for Dudley he remembered the correct address!

After Dudley was captured he was considered 'missing' until the army knew exactly what had happened to him. In the confusion of the evacuation of Greece and then Crete a few weeks later, with almost 4000 New Zealanders becoming prisoners of war and a thousand killed in action, it was 24 May 1941 before two people from the Army visited Win with the news that her younger brother was in fact 'missing'. Not surprisingly, she burst into tears. On 2 August 1941, almost three months after Dudley and a postman had given his sister's address, Win found out that he was alive and a prisoner of war.

Dudley was in hospital for four weeks before he was back at the camp in Corinth. A week later he became part of a mass exodus that traveled

A photograph looking over Stalag 383 and taken from one of the security towers that surrounded the camp.

for three days by train and foot to Dulag 183, a camp in Salonika in northern Greece. From here prisoners were sent by train to permanent camps in Germany. The journey to Salonika and then into the heart of the Third Reich must have felt like an endless nightmare. Men already weakened by illness and a lack of food, were packed like sardines into cattle trucks and then force-marched 40 km over the 1500-m high Braillos Pass as the train tunnel through it had been bombed. When they reached Salonika, they arrived at a camp already holding over 10000 prisoners and conditions worse than those they had left behind at Corinth. After a week here, Dudley was packed into another overcrowded cattle truck for the five-day journey north. It must have been a horrendous trip of dehydration, dysentery and despair.

On 19 June 1941, Dudley arrived at Stalag XVIIID at Marburg, just south of what was then Yugoslavia. He was photographed, fingerprinted, given a prisoner of war number (# 4220) and his clothes were deloused. While it must have made him feel more like a criminal than a captured soldier, there were some advantages to the process. It was here he was registered with the Red Cross and formally placed under the protection afforded by the 1929 Geneva Convention, of which both Germany and Britain were signatories. The Geneva Convention stated that prisoners of war should be treated humanely, adequately fed, and that inspectors from a neutral country (in this case Switzerland) could check on conditions in the camps. It also stated that Officers and Non Commissioned Officers (NCO) – in New Zealand this meant anybody above the rank of private – could not be made to work by the Germans. Dudley had left New Zealand as a corporal and therefore as a Non Commissioned Officer, but when he was sent to Greece his rank reverted back to private. Dudley, a man of many talents, somehow managed to promote himself back to corporal and secure his NCO status while he was at Marburg.

Flyer for Anzac Day and Sports Day at Stalag 383 in April 1943.

However, because the Germans had not yet set up the NCO camps, Dudley still had to spend just over a year at Stalag XVIIID, where he and 200 other men worked on building a road.

In July 1942, fifteen months after his capture in Greece, Dudley was finally moved to an NCO camp and here he bought a notebook and a pencil from a German guard using British cigarettes – the currency of prisoner-of-war camps. He decided to use the notebook to keep a diary of his experiences and observations of life within the camp. For thirty-three months he filled the book with chatty entries, sketches and stick-figure drawings which he called his 'little men'. What makes the diary truly special is the fact that he wrote it to his four-year-old niece Alison, then living in Timaru, 160 km south of Christchurch. So while the diary is a tale of captivity and war, the conditions he endured and the events he lived through are cushioned by being told in a style and language suitable for a child. In August 1945, on his return to Christchurch, Dudley added one last entry, a postscript describing his journey to freedom. He then finished the book with two heartfelt sentences to try and capture for Alison what he had learnt from his wartime experiences: *'Now I shall tell you in three little words what all my travels have taught me, NEVER BE AFRAID. With all the love in the world from Uncle Dudley.'* After embossing *Alison's Book* in gold on the front cover, he at last presented the book to his favourite niece, who was then seven years old.

Dudley never thought he would once again become the book's guardian, but in the mid 1960s Alison became a nun. As part of her vow to separate from worldly goods, she returned the little green book she so highly valued to his possession. Wanting to share the diary, Dudley arranged for photocopies of the book to be made in the early 1990s and gave these to family and friends, before donating *Alison's Book* to Canterbury Museum in Christchurch. Around the same time, he moved into Rannerdale Veterans' Hospital and Home in Christchurch. At 91 he was having difficulties walking, possibly due to being bounced around for decades on his beloved motorcycles, which he rode until he was 85.

Because the diary was written as life was happening and not as reminiscences drawn from later memories, it is a precious account of the day to day realities of life in a prisoner-of-war camp almost seventy years ago. Its survival in the hands of German guards would have been very precarious. They are unlikely to have been amused by Dudley's 'little men' on realising they included drawings of little Germans. Dudley started the book when he was in Spittal Camp, also know as Stalag XVIIIB, situated below the Austrian Alps. Two months later, when the book was only five-pages long, Spittal Camp was disbanded and about 5000 prisoners were sent to the relatively more comfortable Stalag 383 in Hohenfels, Bavaria. Before the shift, everyone and their possessions were thoroughly searched. Somehow the book made it to Stalag 383.

Most of the diary was written between July 1942 and October 1943 and when he was not adding to it, he kept it hidden under the floor of his hut. When Dudley and thousands of other prisoners were marched out of Stalag 383 on 17 April 1945 and away from the approaching American forces, his book could easily have been lost in the chaos. In fact, at one point during the march, a buried bomb was accidentally exploded. The explosion was only metres away from Dudley who was not hurt, but tragically the blast killed one British prisoner of war and badly wounded two others.

Planes fly over Stalag 383 on their way to bomb the German city of Regensberg.

It wasn't only unexploded bombs adding to the tension, that was accentuated by being so close to freedom. The behaviour of fatalistic guards and fanatical members of the SS who also followed the march, combined to make the prisoners feel less secure than when they had been behind the wire fence of Stalag 383. Fortunately, the SS moved on and the guards moved away and soon the Americans guaranteed their safety. On 13 May 1945, after being a prisoner of war for just over four years, Dudley left the tattered Third Reich behind him and landed in Britain.

Stanley Harrison, an Australian bomber pilot with the Royal Air Force who flew liberated British and Commonwealth prisoners from Germany and Belgium to Britain, describes what he saw when they reached Britain, *'Some knelt and kissed the ground; some danced and sang; some were quiet and bewildered; some buttonholed one of the welcoming committee and talked of their POW experiences; some quietly wept'.* While Dudley had been flown to freedom, the trip back to New Zealand was by ship and after just over a month at sea aboard the *Mauritania*, he arrived in Wellington on 4 August 1945 and was back home in Christchurch the following day.

On 5 August 1945 Tom and Win Pollard, and their children John, David and Jim, went down to the Christchurch railway station to meet Dudley. To their dismay he wasn't there. He was 'missing', but only because a friend from Lincoln College had nabbed him first. So, the Pollards returned without Dudley to the family home at 87 Chester Street. Eventually, there was a knock at the door and standing on the step was Dudley in full uniform with a copy of the *Saturday Evening Post* under his arm. He hugged his sister and then walked up to her husband, opened the paper on page three and said, *'Have you see this one Tom?'* It was the comic strip *'Hazel'* syndicated from the United States. They may not have seen him for almost five years, but Dudley wanted it to seem like he had never left. Later, he confessed to David that he had actually planned his casual entrance all along.

Almost five years earlier, when he had last

knocked on the door at Chester Street, life was very different for the then 40-year-old Dudley. When New Zealand joined Britain, France and Australia in declaring war on Germany on 3 September 1939, he was the librarian for Lincoln College, a small agricultural school near Christchurch. A man of many talents and few words, he was also responsible for the college's weather station. On 2 October 1940 Dudley

Private collection of Geoff Hamilton

Timaru, August 23, 1945; the day Dudley gave Alison's Book to Alison.

left a brief note in the weather book as to why he would no longer be able to keep the records. It simply said *'gone to war'*. The week before his 31-year-old brother Selwyn had joined the army. Both men were bachelors, who never married and in an act of solidarity, Dudley enlisted and was soon on his way to Egypt. When he finally returned to his job as librarian in late 1945, his description of his experiences at war was equally succinct: *'Entered Burnham Military Camp October 1940; prisoner of war from the Greek campaign, April 1941: left Germany after 4 years residence, May 1945.'*

As a child in the 1960s, my great uncle Dudley was a regular part of my life, dropping in to see my father, David, or attending the traditional family morning teas held each Saturday at my grandparents' home. Here his sister Win, my grandmother, held court, served freshly baked scones and poured tea from a large teapot clad in a tea cosy. It was during one of these morning teas that Dudley showed me *Alison's Book* and I remember laughing at his 'little men' and thinking how it all seemed like a big adventure. He was a larger than life character and one of my most vivid memories is being taken for a ride on his motorcycle when I was about nine years old. I remember clutching tightly onto his leather jacket to stay on the back of the seat, and how, to my small hands, the leather felt as thick as the hide of an elephant.

The lightness of Dudley's little men and his message to never be afraid are a reminder of the many ways people endured the harsh realities of captivity during World War Two.

Alison's Book

July. 1942.

Dear Alison,

Mummy has told you all about Uncle being a prisoner  so now I must tell you what we do to pass the time. Some of us sometimes play CHESS;

then we have BOXING CONTESTS; 
and quite a lot of us play
BASKETBALL; (see below)

N.W.

← REF, blows whistle.

Every week the KING sends us a packet of 50 cigarettes;

P.O.

but as matches are very scarce it is
sometimes a long time before we can
find someone to give us a light;

Every week too, St. John gives us a RED CROSS
PARCEL;  and just between ourselves darling.
if we didn't get our PARCELS every
week Uncle would have a CROSS
all to himself, like this→ ╬

Auntie Win sent me such a lovely parcel, there was choclate in it and a beautiful pair of boots, they squeak lovely, and all my mates admired them so much;

There is one perfectly horrible thing about being a prisoner, WE HAVE TO DO OUR OWN WASHING AND DARN OUR SOCKS!! Isn't it TERRIBLE?

Every week we have a dance, some of the prisoners dress up as girls, and very lovely they look too. MR DENNIS WHITELY conducts the band—some of the musicians I show you here; the chap weilding the thing like an axe is actually the drummer, he's quite gentle really.

It is very sad dear, but very true, that the Germans open all the tins in our Red Cross Parcels. They do this because so many of the prisoners were saving up the food so they would have lots to eat when they escaped;

←Conductor

← Dancers.

now of course we can't save it up for it would go all smelly. We are not allowed to escape and the Commandant

1944

3.

said that if he caught any naughty men trying to get through the fence they would be shot dead.

Now there were two men who wanted to escape very much so's they could go home and see their Mothers and have a big party with ginger beer and Xmas cake; they didn't want to go through the fence and get all killed, so, one day when the Doctor came in his motor car they waited till the Doctor had gone inside, then they jumped in and scooted off through the gate and the guard didn't know they were prisoners.

The next day when we were on parade the Captain of the guard counted us and found there were two men missing →

"Bring on the BLOODHOUND!" he ordered in a bellowing roar, so away went the fierce BLOODHOUND, sniffing here and sniffing there, and sniffing almost everywhere → after sniffing over all the mountains for about two weeks at last they came to Italy and here the BLOODHOUND was able to sit down and use its hanky, for the search was over.

1962

When the men returned
camp they were put in th
prison cell for two week
and here we find them
at the window, and they ar
so sad, so is the guard
and the BLOODHOUND, for
there is no more chocolate

When the BLOODHOUND and the guard found the escaped men,
they were so tired and hungry after their tramp all over
the mountains, that the men fed them with their chocolate
and brought them back to camp, arriving just in time
for morning tea.

The people are very kind
in this country Alison.
In the winter when theres
lots of snow on the
ground it is very
cold of course for
the birdies, so the
people build little houses
for them and put them up
in the trees. Here we see
the Mother bird coming home
with her children after doing
her shopping.

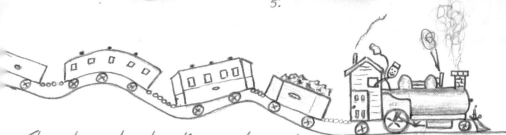

They have lovely trains here, but they haven't got enough of them unfortunately, for there are six million Red Cross Parcels at Geneva, just a few miles away, and we can't get them because there aren't enough trains! Isn't it tough?

And now for some more about our Camp. We have a very good LIBRARY — here you see some of the men leaving with their books — some are light readers and some very heavy readers

We also have a very good barber, he is very busy all day long cutting hair and doesn't charge a penny — here we see him at work

1942

In our bedrooms we sleep in bunks, there are so many of us they have to put us one on top of the other, like this→

If the man on the top starts looking for fleas, or the man in the middle coughs or the man on the bottom sneezes, of course it shakes the bed, and then one man says to the other "Please don't shake the bed Bill" and Bill says, "I'm frightfully sorry old chap" and everybody then goes off to sleep. "Oh Yeah"!

Well dear, on Sept. 18th 1942 we left Spittal camp. After each man had been searched for concealed weapons, such as machine guns, submarines etc. and aids to escape like maps and vanishing cream, we got aboard the train; we spent a couple of days and nights on the train (it was very crowded at night, but it was lovely in the daytime, for this is a very pretty country) we passed many churches. I can't get used to the churches somehow, you see they have a clock up in the steeple, and that makes you think they are Town Clocks until the churchbells ring out calling the good people to service.

There were other churches too, which had a very decided Turkish air about them the roofs being adorned with things like turnips and carrots placed upside down↓

1942

It was a very hot day when the time came to leave the
train, and we had miles and miles to march, up hill and
down, for ever and ever it seemed.

We were welcomed of course, and when we get settled
down I think it will be quite comfy.

At each corner of the camp they have a tower and on this they
have a huge searchlight, which they light up at about 10 p.m. and
it shines on and off all night.

spares →

REGULATOR
INTENSITY OF
BEAM.

REGULATOR
DIRECTION OF
BEAM

CHIEF LIGHTER UPPER

We have a very good bugler, he can't play "Reveille" because he doesn't get up in time:—

I like him best on that soul stiring theme song "Come to the Cookhouse Door Boys" he renders it with a reckless though, well restrained abandon,

* S.P.C.

COOK HOUSE

"LIGHTS OUT!" is not very popular, though we make the best of it

And now Alison I must toddle off to the washhouse and have a shave. I'll draw you a picture of it, and I'd better leave a wall or two out so's you can see all the lovely taps. There are lots of these washhouses scattered about the place, I wish there were as many Cookhouses. You'll spot me with my eyes full of soap groping for the towel.

→ P.T.O

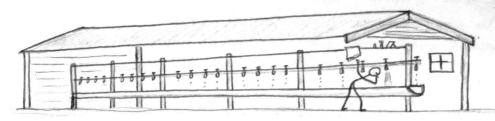

We have very nice little huts, twelve men to a hut; there is a stove of course; when someone lights it to boil up the Billy for a cup of tea, the door and windows come in very handy for letting the smoke out ↙

We have many a quiet game of cards — In this little scene one of the players is a little peeved because his partner left him in One Club and they got FIVE over tricks.

Sept. 24ᵗʰ.
We had some lovely cabbage water for dinner to-day.

The football season has started →

This place is not a scrap like Egypt Alison — I don't know why I mention it — I just thought of it somehow; one of those rare flashes of intuition a chap has sometimes I suppose — anyway you can see for yourself what I mean ↓

I was washing some clothes in the washhouse this morning, and through the window I could see two French "arbiters" digging a hole →

(workers) ↓

an hour or two later when I looked out of the window again, they were still hard at it →

Now that we are getting our 'coal ration' all the chimneys are smoking away furiously; the pall of smoke is like some huge industrial centre in full swing - it brings to mind a little ditty →

> 'Mary had a little lamb,
> Its fleece as white as snow!
> She took it down to Pittsburg,
> And now look at the darn thing!'

The postman came today, but there was no letter for me, so I read some of my old ones. In one that Pauline wrote to me she said that she had knitted some socks using FOUR NEEDLES! how she could be so clever I simply do not know, I thought about it and this is the only way I could think of ↘

It is very sad, but there are not enough Red Cross parcels to go round, so we have to halve one with a mate ↙

I was asked how long I thought the war would go on. I said I didn't know, but was thinking of planting a pine tree so's I could fill in the time bird nesting when it grew up ↙

1962

I have just been thinking dear of the horrors of warfare, and particularly of prison camp life: one of my mates has been waiting eighteen months for a parcel, it came to-day and he got a lovely pair of shoes — both for the LEFT FOOT! Wouldn't that just shake your faith in Father Xmas? I was thinking of the cigarette question too, it is most serious — where the next are coming from, I don't know. I didn't dare think about the Red Cross parcels — far too painful. The Hot Bath question I dwelt on a bit because the camp facilities at present only allows each man to have a bath every six weeks — We'll have to do something about it I think.

Oct 9th. The weather has turned very cold, and while on parade to-day it rained the whole time. I couldn't help but have a few thoughts on the non-utility of our hats as the rain dribbled down my neck.

The Australians have much better hats I think →

Of course, when there are some nice girls about the Aussie wears his hat like this ↘

13.

The Camp Commandant is going to let us go into the forest and chop down some trees for firewood; it should be quite thrilling.

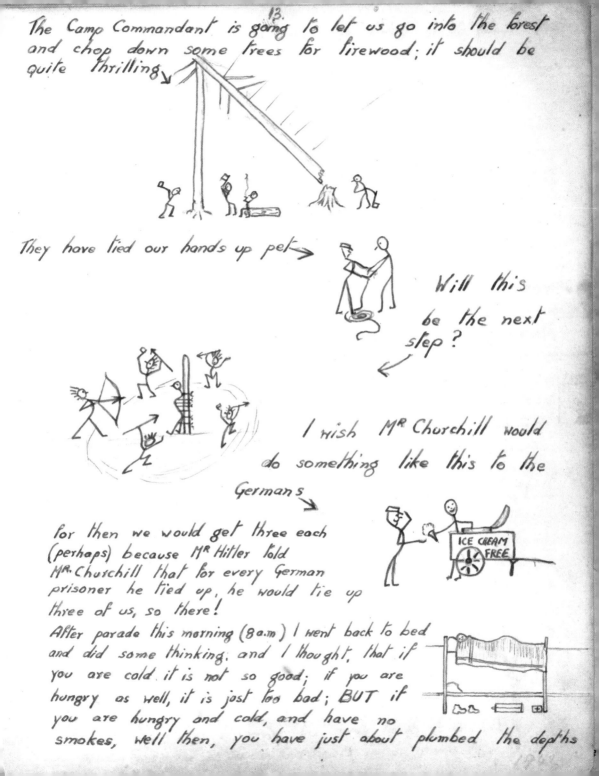

They have tied our hands up pet →

Will this be the next step?

I wish Mr Churchill would do something like this to the Germans →

for then we would get three each (perhaps) because Mr Hitler told Mr Churchill that for every German prisoner he tied up, he would tie up three of us, so there!

After parade this morning (8 a.m) I went back to bed and did some thinking, and I thought, that if you are cold it is not so good; if you are hungry as well, it is just too bad; BUT if you are hungry and cold, and have no smokes, well then, you have just about plumbed the depths

of human misery — there is only one thing to do about it —
just go right on being cheerful →

because tea-leaves make but a
poor substitute for tobacco;
likewise grass & coffee grounds.
Brewed tea leaves collected and
dried, and brewed again, even
with the addition of sugar, do
not, and can not, even with the
aid of a very powerful imagination incline one to the
belief that one is drinking anything but warm muddy
water.

Oct. 19th

    I am not very often moved to poetic fervour Alison, but this
morning I was inspired to exclaim; Is things what they seem?
It is true enough, thousands of   Or does visions hang around?
parcels have arrived.

We eat again, and smoke TOBACCO! I feel almost as good as if I
were back in Cairo watching the girlies dance

The Military Police were never far away though from
these places—this one is tired and wants to go home.

Now that the parcels have arrived a certain difficulty arises re cooking facilities; some of the men have added ovens to their stoves; the idea is fundamentally sound, and I am going to submit to my roommates a plan for improving our stove, on somewhat the following lines

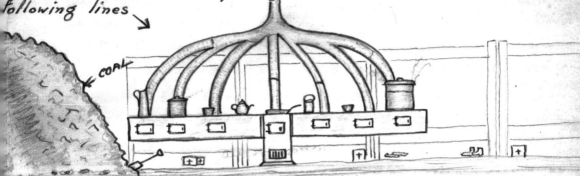

COAL

Oct. 24th. As you can see from the blankets and washing on the line we have had a lot of wet weather — this is the first fine day for a week —

Oct 25th. We had two air-raid alarms last night, no bombs were dropped, which is a good thing I think, what with having our hands tied up and one thing and another, we don't want any further unpleasantness; if you think my dear that this life is a joke, just try ironing a shirt with a hot brick in a biscuit tin, or making pancake fritters without a frying pan — it's just as easy to slam a revolving door. We have a German mouse in our room now, I notice he did not make an appearance until our Red Cross Parcels arrived, so he's got a bit of sense; for my part he's quite welcome to stay, because I don't like Jerry rations either. I suppose some super German, "stuka" cat will get him sometime though.

From a little booklet of cheer sent to Prisoners of War I
quote the following - it is from the Persian:-

"Tell me, gentle traveller, who hast wandered through the
world, and seen the sweetest roses blow, and brightest,
gliding rivers —— of all thine eyes have seen, which
is the fairest land?

Child, shall I tell thee where nature is most blest
and fair? It is where those we love abide.
Though that space be small, ample is it above
kingdoms; though it be a desert, through it
runs the river of Paradise, and there are the
enchanted bowers."

You may take it from me little one, those Persian chaps
knew a thing or two. I'll quote another, though I don't like it:-

"Lord, Thou knowest I shall be very busy this day
I may forget Thee. Do not Thou forget me."
(SIR JACOB ASTLEY BEFORE THE BATTLE OF EDGEHILL — Oct. 1642)

it sounds too much like asking Him to keep an eye on the
office while you go to lunch.

Oct. 27th A great day! two letters from Auntie Eva, and a
cigarette parcel:→

I heard a plane overhead and saw
a chap looking for it →

another FIVE LETTERS to-day. It is simply wonderful, I received
though they do unsettle me; I start thinking of home and
how lovely it would be to see you all again. I can
imagine the Commandant saying to me, "Dudley, you
have been a very good boy so you can go home, and
take lots of lollies home to Alison."

The thing to decide now
is the quickest way to get there,
an areoplane would be the best
of course →

or if I couldn't get a plane
a very fast motor-boat would do

but even if I couldn't get a plane or a motor boat, I'd
surely be able to get hold of a row-boat

and if it took a long, long time, and I looked like this
when I arrived →   and you looked like this →

I would get there.

1942

The football season is still in progress →

It is not easy to get suitable
firewood here; all the spare beds, bed-boards,
and other wooden fixtures went long ago.
If one does happen to see anything lying about, well, one ma
tidy things up →

This chap is not making plans for escape, he is trying to
think of a four letter word starting with "L" meaning
"to adore" →

Because I am a New Zealander Alison, a lot of my mates call me "Kiwi". I
I don't mind that a bit for the Kiwi is a very wise birdie. At one time
used to fly about all day catching insects so's he'd have strength enough
fly about all the next day to catch more insects. He woke up one
morning and thought about the matter and decided it was silly
go tearing about all day, when he could pick up worms for
practically nothing, so he turned over and went to sleep again.
When he woke up it was late afternoon, and all the worms were
gambolling and playing about, so he just strolled among them,
joined in the fun, and incidentally had a jolly good tea. He's bee
eating worms for so long now he has
lost the use of his wings altogether,
that doesn't matter, cause if he did
want to fly he could go up in an
areoplane, couldn't he?

1942

I don't know who wrote those words,
        " O Paradise! O Paradise!
         'Tis weary waiting here."
but as I made the toast this morning
I could not help thinking how well the
Poet expresses most of our hopes and
fears in this life.

Nov. 5th.

Another parcel
of cigarettes to-day.
I hardly know how
to take them.

STORE

200

Nov. 13th. Another wonderful day — nine letters!! In one I learn
that Pauline is keen on skating — which brings back
memories of my efforts, I was pretty good too, I never
exactly won any races, nor did I jump any of the hurdles
they used to put on the floor, because I was too busy
mastering the "Waltz", which I was taking on when I could go
backwards without falling forwards, and forwards without
falling backwards. I had just got the whole thing worked
out (it was ridiculously easy, really) when the Rink closed down,
still, as you can see I can appreciate some of the game's finer
points →

1942

On Nov.15ᵗʰ the first snow came floating prettily down. Now in th
land the gentle tinkle of the sleigh bells will be heard; overh
the roar of the war birds, and their eggs will stain the
whiteness with red; and somewhere the Bells will peal forth
the glad tidings of a great victory; and I am glad Aliso
you are not old enough to understand all this.

Nov 19ᵗʰ

I wrote a letter to Colleen to-day and that reminded
of when I used to have to wheel her father about in the
pram — we all toured majestically forth in that pram at
one time or another—Auntie Dods used to push me; Auntie
Eva pushed Auntie Dods; Aunt Cassie pushed Aunt Eva and
Dad pushed the lot of us; there is more to it than tha
but summarised the position was something like this

Nov. 25ᵗʰ
We now have a Table Tennis Set, and while the balls
hold out we'll continue to have a lot of fun

Dec. 15ᵗʰ
I have been thinking again — in the same old place
it really is the best place too — though I
have, on one or two occasions, rather gained
the impression from remarks let slip by

my mates that it is the home of the born lazy - that I
run the risk of dying there, and that the table is the place
for meals - these and other thinly veiled innuendoes leave
me still snug and warm; for what's the use? if you do get
up, and go for a walk, the ground is so hard and frozen
you run the risk of breaking something →
or else it's so muddy it takes an hour to
scrape your boots clean when you come

inside. →   They have issued us with "clogs"; they are
                        warm, and being made of wood sooner or
                          later find their way into the stove; They
are useful in other ways too. Back at Marburg a Frenchman
was being coaxed along by having a rifle jabbed into his
back, he didn't like it, so he whipped off one of his clogs
and crowned the wicked guard.
He was sent to jail of course for this
act of violence, but who cares, having
fallen in the water, about getting wet?

Rough? Who? Me??

Well, I started off to
tell you that I was
thinking again; not
about anything in particular of course, but just letting
my thoughts idle along. I noticed one of my mates
put on the "electric kettle" or "immersion heater" for a
cuppa tea, and that started me thinking about being
far away from Mother and the necessity of invention,
It really is remarkable what can be done with a few
odds and ends; this heater of ours for instance!
It is merely two empty sugar tins fixed on a
stick, a couple of wires are fastened on to the tins,
the other end of the wires being attached to the

electric light wires and things (if I grow too technical
Daddy will explain) it takes no time at all to boil
the water, especially if you can get a jugful of ho...
from the cookhouse

→ Water from Cookhouse   Dixie   Heater

Another type in use is made from half a dixie (B.A.
it is most useful, can be used as an 'iron' for doing one
hankies or as a 'toaster', besides boiling the water.

My own contribution to
P.O.W. Science is a
modest "Nutmeg Grater" —
merely a tin opened
out, a lot of holes made
with a nail, and there
you are! It is handy for reducing biscuits to powder, or
mashing potatoes.

Some of the men   If, when using one is no
(Confidence Men, W.O's and   careful, one is liable to lose
suchlike) have proper   skin off one's knuckles, by Jo
                                     iron bedsteads, these provide strips
of hard steel, which, with the requisite number of teeth filed
out, make excellent sawblades for cutting up beds, shelves ec...
I don't know where   the file came from, or how th
owner managed to   conceal it through the
dozens of searches   there have been for suchlike
instruments, but there it is, nothing, absolutely nothing
could surprise me here; if someone was to tell me that
in a hut in "C" Lager they had a cow which they were
milking, I would naturally enquire whether they milked it...
machine or by hand. The Concert Party have an "Arc-
     * British Army Issue.   1941

light" for use in their shows (with dimmer) they used the lead out of pencils at first, but found that the carbon from old batteries was best. Many serviceable wood and paper burning stoves have been made out of milk tins →

I have seen in action a lantern for projecting pictures out of books on to a screen. This was used in one of the many "classes" arranged by the studious. Many excellent "civvy" suits have been tailored out of blankets, the dye being obtained from pills procured from the M.I. room. When making an attempt at escape a "civvy" suit is most useful. I have heard of a camera being made; I have seen a proper lathe 4" centre; I hear of an electric mouse trap; and I have seen dainty picture frames and fancy belts made of cellophane. No doubt there are many other things I don't know about — as I hear of them I'll make further notes.

Now here is a thing which looks alright in story books but as a means of escape is simply rotten — I've tried it, and it just doesn't work — I should have known anyway. it isn't likely they would issue us with brooms like these if they were any good, is it?

HONK! KONK!

JANUARY FIRST - 1943.

As you can well imagine dear, the possible duration of the war, and the exact date of our release from chains, tinned foods, and an horizon surrounded by barbed wire, gives rise to much speculation, many and varied are the conjectures in circulation, and equally so the modus operandi employed to ascertain same. Now, I am not seeking to deride the honest efforts of those truth seeker, who delve deep into Spiritualizm; or of those embryo Prophet. who seek their inspiration in the pages of the Bible, in the rocks of the Pyramids, in Necromancy; or that host of diligent workers who dig up an occasional pearl in Dream land; I respect them, but I still think my method just as good as theirs, if not a jolly sight better by a long shot. Anyway, you shall judge for yourself. Follow closely, while I take you deep into the mysteries of Numerology ! The one and only true Science !!

```
            original Army Number   15079
               "      P.O.W.  "     4220
            new     P.O.W.  "      1687
                         Total    20986
           subtract year of Birth  1900
                                  19086
           Subtract present Age       42
                                  19/0/44
```

Now here is where the Science of Numerology comes in; I have now the date—the 19th of "nought" month 1944 — 1944 is too far away, and you can't have a "nought" mont

```
so I take the → 19044
subtract "one"         1
                   19043
put "one" back         1
                   19143
```

I then put the 'one' back, displacin the 'nought', which miraculously gives me the 19th of January 1943. which just suits me fine.

Jan. 7th 1943.

We now have a "Dart Board". It was made with innumerable (30 or 40 to be exact) empty Red Cross boxes cu into strips and wound round and round. Several biscuit

Goodbye Europ

tins and a few odds and ends of wire and a lot of patience, plenty of advice and a bit of luck completed the job – it's a "whizzer." The game was new to us at first, but we are now learning our way about – the terminology employed is, to the novice, just pure jargon, but after you've been in <u>"Annie's Room"</u> and the <u>"Mad-house"</u> a few times, and been in need of <u>"Bed and breakfast"</u> you begin to appreciate the subtleties of the game. One thing I like about it, it does not cramp style; one is _{not} bound by rigid law to conform to a particular "stance" or "grip", as in golf for instance, the only thing insisted on, is that one does not put ones <u>"feet in the water"</u>, in other words one must <u>"toe the line"</u>. Individual styles of play make for colourful play I think, Jock is a rugged player, and brings a breath of the "wide open space."

one of his   spears went into my dixie – it was on the shelf 3 ft. 9" away from the bull at the time. Jimmy is a cautious player, can't forget his 'bridge' and 'finesses' too much

Charlie is nonchalant, but always manages to get there, he's a lightening calculator too.

We have a few dainty players also →

Nothing out of the way distinguishes my stance or play though I do at times effect a marvellous recovery from seemingly impossible positions.

There are plenty of hazards in the game; tea-making, shaving, boot polishing etc., usually commences with the start of a game, one of these days an ear or two will be pinned to the wall.

In 'Football' to decide who has the opening advantage a coin is tossed, the same as in Australias' National Pastime "Two-up" in most card games the cards are "cut"

but in "Darts" the one who throws his dart nearest the board has the advantage. *

Planes of all types and sizes are continually passing over our camp; some just crawl along, others come with a screaming roar, and are out of sight before one can get to the door to have a 'look.' I am not greatly interested in planes myself, saw too many at too close quarters in Greece for my liking ➜

* This applies to Colonials only.

1943

146

A letter from N.Z. in 36 days! That is certainly hurry upping. The Tommies of course can write home and receive an answer in just about that time the Aussies, well, their mail is such, that some declare it comes by Pony Express overland

and then by Ye Olde English clipper service

March. 6th.

I have been very fortunate this week Alison I have had letters from everyone at home and a cigarette parcel.

We have had lovely weather for a fortnight, and now it is snowing again — us soldiers can take

I am more than convinced, after a perusal of our Camp newspaper that far more millions of tons of shipping have been sunk than could have ever existed. Even allowing for a pardonable, exaggerated pride in this marvellous achievement, I am at a loss to understand how millions of men and their equipment are still being transported to and fro over the billowing main. I am forced to the conclusion that museums have been ransacked; Yacht Clubs coerced and even private owners prevailed upon to help keep the convoys moving.

<u>March. 12th</u>   Almost every day we have air raid alarms.

I recently received two cigarette parcels from N.Z. and have had letters from every member of the family. The Red Cross parcels are arriving regularly, so everything in the garden is lovely.

1943

"In the Springtime, when a young man's fancy, lightly turns to
thoughts of love " was certainly not written of "gefangeners".
No jolly fear. All we can think of when the sap begins to rise
is how to get through the wire, over it, or under it. I have
not yet heard of anyone making a pair of wings and flying over
but there is yet time.

Two fences about
six feet apart. Loosely
coiled wire in middle.

I heard of a chap in another camp who crawled on his hands
and knees down a long drain, when he got to the end there was
a guard with a big dog waiting for him. The guard 'sooled' the
dog on to him, so all the chappie could do was to turn round and
crawl back, with the dog nibbling at his pants all the way. (It is
too painful to illustrate) He had a large scale escape here the other
night, I believe about a dozen actually got away, though, had they
kept quieter, at least three times that number would have been
successful. It was pretty general knowledge about the camp that a
tunnel was being dug; but the actual location and date of
inauguration was kept most secret, and not known except by
a select 400 or so. A good deal of hard work must have been
put into its construction, as it was 60 to 80 yards long, and had
to be boarded up to prevent falls of earth; one chap was nearly
buried alive in one fall. Electric light wires were conducted down
its entire length, and to keep the air circulating (in another
tunnel at another camp some workers nearly lost their lives through
foul air) a fan was attached to a gramaphone (kindly donated
by the Red Cross) It was one man's job to keep it wound up

My first intimation that the escape was on, was on being awakened by rifle shots. The Camp Commandant took a lenient view of the proceedings; no reprisals, so it won't be long before another general evacuation is planned. If I had a lot of German money, could speak the language, and had the push of a life insurance salesman, I'd have a shot at it myself.

<u>April. 8th</u>
Another cig. parcel. Whoopee!

<u>April 14th</u>. And another one!! Two whoopees!!
The weather is hot, glorious. I have been wondering if our Senior Officers will carry on with this little courtesy when we get out of captivity?

Not very likely. What!

<u>April. 24th</u>
It's about time Alison I put some more news in our little book. All interest at present is focussed on the Anzac Day celebrations, and Easter festivities in general. This afternoon a big sports programme commences with a display of boxing and wrestling; then to-morrow, there is a big day of field events, following the Dawn Service and March Past. The weather promises to hold good, and a happy time should be enjoyed by all. Our hosts have given every assistance in making preparations, though I have not heard of their suggesting a big Cross Country Event — this is a pity, it would save such a lot of trouble — do you know, some of our boys dug a lovely new tunnel, but they made a miscalculation in the length of it somewhere or other, and when they crawled forth from the hole, there they were, standing between the two fences!! Outside the wire are lovely grazing lands for sheep,

and as you know it is at this time of the year when all the little lambs are born. Now, one little lambkin managed somehow to get through the wire into the parade ground, immediately, one of our men pounced upon it

and bore it off to his hut, calling to his mate to go and find some mint. While his mate was getting the mint sauce ready, the good shepherd had missed his lamb and went to the Commandant.

the Commandant, without the slightest trace of strain or fluster listened to the shepherds tale and promptly ordered out the guard to make a search

I am very sorry dear, but I'm afraid I cannot tell you just what happened— whether lamby skipped back to mother, or whether it rightly and justly finished up as cutlets — but I'm afraid that unless they put it into the coal bucket and covered it well over with coal, or stuffed it up the chimney, or alternatively, were eloquent enough to convince the guard that they had received it in a parcel from home, or again, that it had attacked them, and they had acted in self defence — that the dear thing has by now, been gathered into the fold once more.

Well, the weather, like our mail, the electric light and Red Cross parcels, cannot be relied upon, it is now raining. I went to the sports arena and saw a wrestling bout, but as it was so wet and the bout so tame I came home. I like the wrestling they have in civvy street, which usually ends like this ➤ _____ which reminds me, saw a good boxing bout not so long ago, and I'm sure my man would have won if he'd only kept cool and not lost his head:

I like sports, especially football; they play a lot here too, it keeps the boys fit and gives the medical staff something to do. This is the sort of thing that puts the goalkeeper on a par with the referee for popularity →

← Net made of string from Red Cross parcels.

Hockey too is very popular →

April 26th. Easter Monday 1943

Our Anzac Day celebrations went through with a swing. The Dawn was on time for the Service, which was short. At 10 a.m. the parade left the sports ground, headed by the Anzacs. Representatives from England, Scotland, Ireland, Wales, Isle of Man, Canada, South Africa, and Cyprus, followed in that order. Over 100 last war veterans brought up the rear. We swung along past Coney Island, turned left at the washhouse, and headed for the 'Two-up' ring, where the Band was playing martial airs. Opposite the Band, on the basket ball ground stood MAJOR G. NEILL, taking the salute. We 'eyes righted' smartly, then carried on by a circuitous route which

1943

brought us back to our starting point, where we broke off.
About a thousand or more took part in the actual procession, the
other two thousand or so, stood smartly to attention in rapt
admiration as we filed silently by. It was all very well managed
and I thought, very impressive. The sports programme was
immediately got under way. A very nice boy in blue pants
won the 100 yards

and this is how the competitors in the High Jump saw the S.African
pull it off

the same chap stepped over a few hurdles quicker than anyone e

then I'm bothered if he didn't putt the shot so far they had to
put fieldsmen out

Digging so many tunnels must have given the boys the idea of digging for profit, anyway. almost everyone in town this season has his allotment to water, weed and watch. These two seem to have grave suspicions that something might be coming up:

The Town Planning and Beautifying Association has been encouraging the men to improve their lot in life — some have done really well:

the paint, to represent the bricks, was obtained by grinding to powder some real bricks and mixing with water; the blue paint I think, is dye from the packing in our Red Cross parcels, likewise, the yellow for the curtains. The grass is turf lifted from the back lawn, and the crazy paving is concrete slabs from the alleged swimming pool now under construction.

1943.

<u>May. 5</u>th.

   There are six of these towers strategically placed about the camp. It is almo
impossible to move away from the hut after dark, without being picked up by the
searchlight. The light from this one shines directly on to my bed; after a hard da
it is very annoying to have lights flashing on and off all night, but a few towels
judiciously arranged fixes things.

FLASH !!!   The Commandant, is alleged to have stated that he is
pleased at the interest shown by the men in their gardening, but is afraid that
they will not be here to reap the benefit. Now, what does that mean? Is it possible
thinks the war will be over? Is it likely? Not much !

1943

There are five of these buildings in camp. One is permanently used as a theatre, another, houses the library, classrooms etc., while another, is used for storing Red Cross and civvy parcels, the other two are always in use for something or other. The Red Cross store I am sorry to say is as empty as our stove. Mac, our Confidence Man has the wires humming between here and Geneva imploring the immediate despatch, by special trains or the entire German Air Force if necessary, sufficient parcels to ensure a minimum of four per man if they expect our Empire Day sports fixture to be a success. That'll shake 'em.

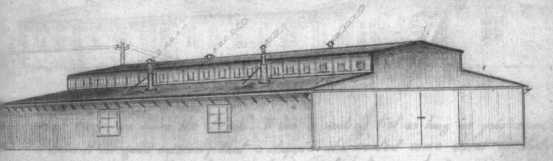

We have an artist in this room. In the good old days when cigarettes had some value as a medium of exchange, he must have swopped some "Gold Flakes" for a box of coloured chalks, anyway, ever since, he's had the walls covered with this sort of thing, tantalising isn't it? Hardly cricket though!

You can take it from me, a starving man does not from choice read cookery books to beguile the time, nor does he gaze at coloured illustrations of sirloins of beef, and custards and things. So why do it, Ces, old man?

May 6th FLASH!!! True Rumour has it that next week the Germans are going to cut our rations in half. Cripes!

1963

This is our "Cookhouse". It is a double barrelled affair, there being two complete kitchens housed in the one building. Our own men do the cooking, and are they good? I'll say! Do you know, this particular cookhouse turns out over 8,000 litres of hot water per day!! and some of it boiling!!!

*

And here we have the "Boob". It has a waiting list as long as your arm. I have it on good authority that a chappie who wanted some quiet to study, changed places with a chap who had 14 days to serve! And this appeared on the Notice Board at Marburg under List of Punishments, March 21st 1942: "The English P.o.W. Hodges, for laughing scornfully when the Camp

Commandant asked the English N.C.O's on Feb. 22nd if they would volunteer for work. 14 days rigorous imprisonment."

* "Boob" — Prison. It is full of nasty little cells.

I nearly went to school to-day, but was afraid I might be put in the corner, so stayed home. Quite a number of Colleges in 'civvy street' might envy our curriculum it embraces almost everything from Agricultural Science to Engineering, and that reminds me, Abe had three fried eggs for tea the other night, he traded ¼ lb of chocolate and two cakes of soap for them.

May 9th T.C.

This is one of our many wash-houses. Sharp on eight of a morning as the bugle goes for parade, a wild stampede commences to these points. I've tried to show what the inside looks like somewhere else. Because you see a chimney don't for one moment think that it has anything to do with hot water. I don't know what it is for – propaganda perhaps.

May 12th.

A letter from home dated March 16th!!! They can certainly get a move on when they like.

May 13th. Air alarm last night 1-30 am - "all clear" 2.am. There has been another tunnel fiasco and as a result there is only one wash-house and one cook-house in operation, for 4000 men! The tunnel would have been a great success I think if they had chosen some other spot where the water main couldn't have interferred – anyway, they didn't have to stick a pick into it.

1943

May 14ᵗʰ.
They filled our swimming pool to-day and it is 100 %, efficient,
except of course that it is not long enough, and there is no diving board, which
perhaps is just as well for someone would be sure to alight on somebody,
it is so crowded always.

May 25ʳᵈ.
Jerry has rather a suspicious mind, almost every day he puts a couple
of men in our midst who have nothing to do but snoop round, see what they ca
find in the way of dart boards, electric fittings, wireless sets etc. and what th
can hear. It is our own fault if we are taken unawares by a visit of these gentry, for
our bugler from some advantageous position notes their entry, and plays a
warning tune — on their departure he sounds the all clear.

May. 25ᵗʰ.
Received letters from Kath, Pauline, Ruff, Doff, and Dods, all
posted about March 20ᵗʰ. Good going! Jerry gave date of Tunis
finals as May 13ᵗʰ. This week the whole camp is to be medically
examined and innocculated, ha, ha!

41.

I have tried here to show you a view in one of the cookhouses — I've had to remove a whole host of cooks and enough steam to send the Queen Mary to N.Z. so's you could see anything at all; We always have potatoes for dinner, they are steamed. and I think the gear for cooking rather neat.

↙

Here is a view of the pans which fit into the boilers, there are four of them here, sixteen for the whole camp, not enough either the way the men keep rolling in from all over Germany.

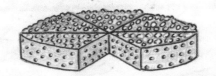

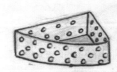

May. 27th.

A letter from Dods dated April 1st. The mail gets faster and faster.

1963

May 28th.
I did some washing yesterday and this I hope looks something like the place where I did it—at the back of the chimney is another boiler, which helps to provide a continual supply of boiling water.

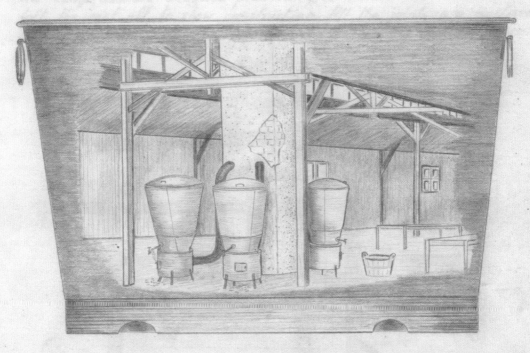

In Greece we had a mobile laundry unit. I never saw it, but I believe that it was one of the best of its kind in existence—Monday held no terrors for the MOBILE LAUNDRY and FORWARD DECONTAMINATING UNIT. Their outfit cost £80.

they have about 19 trucks – the heaviest being about 8 tons – and their record output for 24 hours is 58,000 pieces!

June 7th.

    Here we have a "Hot-plate". There are two of them so far in the camp, and are designed presumably, to relieve the cookhouses. I have left the roof off to show construction. All the joints are mortised, not a nail is used. Scot's Fir is the timber – you can see that for yourself anyway.

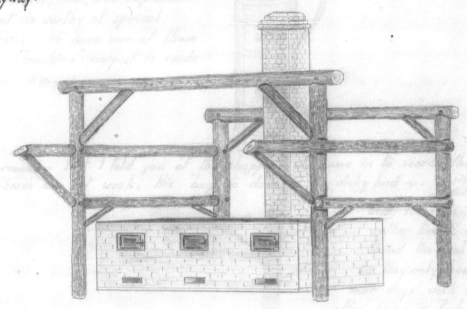

Wooden peg fixing tenon ➜

June 9th.
    They have a tile roof on now

June 9th.
    The boys instead of going to bed at "lights out" have been loitering round outside, and the guards don't like it much because they think they might be planning to escape, so last night a guard said to two men "Go to bed" and just to show he wasn't joking fired a couple of shots over their heads, this evidently inspired other guards, for

guns went popping off in all directions. No damage was done beyond spoiling our sleep. Our swimming pool has been put to an original and novel use, several chaps being ducked last night.

June 10th.

I said I would report inventions as they come to my notice, but they are so many I must refrain; still, this improvised tea-pot is worthy of special mention. We have one of these in our "combine" only it is made of four tins.

This tea leaf container fits into the top

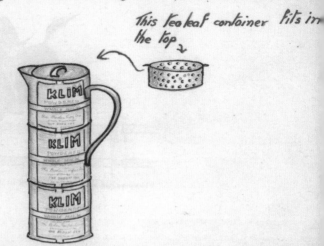

You remember that I told you of the choppies who come in to search the camp? well, here's one at work. His "bag" to date is one dicky bird →

and three tunnels. It was rather bad luck that he found the last tunnel, for they only had about more days work to do after being a fortnight on job. They had lights and air circu system; went under pipe lin and over rocks, everything w set, and then 'snoopy' had come along. It'd make a stro man weep.

June 18th.

Our camp occupies one corner of a vast training centre for Jerry troops; through the wire we often see them on manoeuvres, marching all over the place, dragging big guns about, popping off machine guns and having a fine old time generally. A number of

The officers prance around an bonny steeds, looking very fine, and no doubt feeling very fine - this chappie is in a hurry for his dinner I think →

June 19th

I have mentioned several times the construction of tunnels, and their detection by Jerry; this little scene depicts what should happen and probably what will happen the moment Jerry relaxes his vigilance. How far they might get if they were successful in getting away is another matter. Two chaps from the last break were picked up in a theatre queue in Munich!

June 19th

A parcel - choc. pyjamas, braces etc., - great!
Finals of Empire Day sports yesterday - Kiwis provided great thrill in Tug-of-war - an excellent show.
It is raining steadily, and has been for about a month, off and on.

46.

June 21st.

Here's the view through our window, I have been looking at it for nearly a year now, and I'm terribly fed up with it.

It's the view through the open gates I want.

June 27th.

To pass the time pleasurably and profitably Alison is our chief concern, as I think maybe I mentioned before; here are one or two methods I should have told you about long ago → this chap along with his mates, put in their time making and sailing boats in the swimming pool; another has some pigeons another a hen →

while yet another has a rabbit → or perhaps I should say, had a rabbit - I have an idea that bunny contributed towards a stew; quite a number too, play marbles!

July 6th.

The Commandant is reported to have instructed the guards to take no notice, and refrain from laughing at the prisoner's antics in the camp; the strain of three years confinement he thinks, is beginning to tell. Of course, most Jerries think the English are mad. The Commandant of another Stalag said; "He can manage the French, the Russians and the Poles, but the English, ach! they are mad. This idea has grown I think, from the Englishmans' reluctance to take a blow without hitting back, and several of our men have been killed and many injured for refusing to work under conditions which did not conform to their ideas of Justice, fair play and their own Trade Union Rules. Mind you, when our Commandant, who is a Gentleman, sees men sailing toy boats all day, playing Indians and Cowboys, marbles; games such as cricket, without wickets, bat or ball:

and a tough Sgt. Major pulling a tin round on a string in lieu of a train:

and when on parade the list of punishments is read out, and each mans sentence is greeted by resounding cheers, it is hardly surprising if he shows a little concern for our mental condition.

1943

July. 11th Sunday - raining. S.L.

Aug. 17th   Great excitement to-day - saw an air raid! The whole camp was o to see our planes pass by to give Regensburg a do over. One plan crashed in flames, and several stray pieces of metal came whizzing past us to find a lodging in some of our huts.

Aug. 28   Another raid on Nuremburg last night, an hours pyrotechnic display.

Sept. 1st   Another raid. Munich I think.

Sept. 8th   Air raid alarms are so frequent I shall not record them. Last night came news of the capitulation of Italy.

Oct. 12th   Protected personnel (Red cross) left to-day for HOME!! In evening first batch of Repats. left. Last night great excitement, guard shot and wounded one of our chaps. He got too near the fence.

MARCH. 23 1944.   I must break this long silence my dear; it is nearly six months since I drew you some little men. In this sketch I have tried to show you what I think happens when the air-raid alarm wails forth. You see a weird animal (the Sirenus, of the Klaxon species) in a box, its tail is extremely sensitive and the lightest touch causes it to yell with rage — well, you can see for yourself what happens

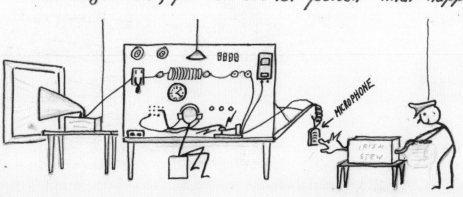

an expert electrician might observe a minor error or two in my "circuit" but we can't be worried.

July 21st Plenty air raid alarms recently. Saw our planes to-day, some shot down.

Rumours fly around since news of abortive attempt on Hitlers life.

During the winter, when we received a coal ration, a great deal of it was so poor, something had to be done about it; our "Forced Draft Heatless Smoker" was the result, after much painstaking toil and research. In general principle it might be said to resemble the common blacksmiths' forge, but a little more, than merely a cursory glance will reveal details of construction, and such a lovely scorn of mechanical laws, nay! defiance I should say, as would make a blacksmiths' puny effort seem childish. Here it is anyway

The Johnny with his hand on wheel turns vigorously, thus propelling, per medium of boot-lace, the fan concealed in klim-tin; the fan drives the air through two cocoa tins, which are cunningly connected with the fire-box, also made of tin, and the joint effort of these highly technical and complicated parts is to produce a huge rattle and a lot of smoke; it must be worth the effort though, for there are hundreds in the camp.

Nov. 1st. 1944.

Life goes on — it's a habit it has — and we are still, more or less, making the best of things. When you spot a chap cleaning up things from under his bed, and going through his pockets for the fifteenth time, you can bet the cigarettes are getting short

"butt" dropped, the winter before last. 1944

Now, there is a little matter which is causing no little concern, and that is the effect of the R.A.F.'s activities on our food and fuel supply It is no wonder we are on half a parcel a week, when these mosquitoes start dropping their bombs on trains and things. (NOTE: Bombs are by nature uppish, but strange to say, it's the downward journey and subsequent bump that spoils things so.)

Then there is the Mustang; he's an American product I believe, beloved by the cowboy →
. he doesn't help matters much

1944

But everybody, according to their emotional nature, got a surge of feeling, more or less, when they heard that the church which somebody had ordered from Geneva, had turned up safely.

The question is —

Is one Church enough?

Nov. 20th

WHOA! I mean HALT!!

There is a definite feeling of optimism once more prevalent in camp. The question now is "When do you think it will end?" or better still "Do you think it will be over by Xmas?" which is a decided improvement on "Will it ever end?"

Xmas Day. Last month's optimism is not quite so evident to-day.

New Years Day. 1945: And still less to-day. Parcels, all done!

1945

Somebody who wasn't there will write an Heroic Ode about
this event I suppose.

Jan. 12ᵗʰ. Still no sign of any Red Cross parcels and further
cuts in rations promised – the coal ration is meagre wh
we get a lot – we've used all our spare wood, but in the
several cross-beams supporting the roof have a tidy
reserve. It is cold of course, but very comforting to kno
that the shortest day is behind us and that somewhere
ahead lies the longest.

1945

Is it any wonder our boys dig tunnels when the
Jerries build gates like this to keep us in
↓

Down by the Old Garden Gate.

Jan. 18th. Well, Alison we've had a grand week; first
of all the weather has been milder - it was only 5° below
yesterday; then our engineers got busy and threw out the
Jerry stove and built one nearer to our heart's desire —
instead of about four, the whole fourteen of us can
now gather round the fire; three cigarette parcels
                                            have come

into the room – we smoke again; our rations have been considerably increased; Joe is putting in a big push that looks as if it might succeed in pushing me right home to you; and now some parcels have arrived and we are to be issued with one between three !! and last, but not the least, our parades are now held at 2 p.m. instead of at 8=

Jan. 23rd

Feb. 24th. And so the Turks have at last decided to take up arms – it's just about time the infidels realized their obligations and gave us Christians a hand with the bombing.

March 1st. With the situation something like this. ↑

196

Just a few more little men Alison and my story is finished. On April 17th 1945 about 3000 of us set off on a march away from the Americans who were drawing closer and closer every day — here we are → most of us had to carry our belongings

but quite a few had appropriated prams, carts, carriages— anything in fact that had a wheel.

On May 1st the Yanks set us free, and on May 10th flew us to Brussels. On the 13th we set foot on English soil at Guildford. The great day came on July 3rd. when we stepped on board the great ship Mauratania at Liverpool, which then took us to Panama, then Pearl Harbour THEN to N.Z. and you know the rest dear.

Now I shall tell you in three little words what all my travels have taught me, NEVER BE AFRAID.

With all the love in the world from.
                                    Uncle Dudley.

over —

Epilogue

'Nothing, absolutely nothing could surprise me here; if someone was to tell me that in a hut in "C" Lager they had a cow which they were milking, I would naturally enquire whether they milked it by machine or by hand.'
From *Alison's Book*, December 15, 1942

Dudley (at the end of the table with his head against his hand) and hut mates in Stalag 383.

From September 1942 until April 1945 Dudley lived with 11–14 other men in a 9-m by 4-metre hut with double bunks down the side, a stove, a table and stools. As he wrote in 1942, *'Who has less privacy than a goldfish in a bowl?'*. Of course, this was the reality of captivity for the 5000 men, including 320 New Zealanders who lived in one of the Lagers that collectively contained 400 huts in Stalag 383. However, from all accounts, Stalag 383 was one of the best camps in Germany and the Commandant, Oberst Felix Aufhammer mostly let the men run the camp themselves. The elected camp leader or 'confidence man' was Squadron Quartermaster Sergeant David Mackenzie whose job it was to negotiate the welfare of the men with the Commandant. Apparently, both were masons and got on very well. The Commandant was described as, *'first class, fair, impartial and equipped with a good sense of humour'*. For example, he gave escaped prisoners who were recaptured a prison sentence based on how far they got away from the camp. The greater the distance, the less the prison sentence!

When the Americans arrived at Stalag 383 on 22 April 1945, the senior British officers that were still at the camp gave the Commandant glowing testimonials.

Because Stalag 383 was a Non Commissioned Officers (NCO) camp the prisoners could not be forced to work and how they filled in time was up to them. The currency of cigarettes allowed the men to barter amongst themselves for things that had come in parcels from home or that they had made themselves within the camp. However, with cigarettes, chocolate and soap, they could bribe the German guards to get them almost anything they wanted except their freedom. While a mechanically-milked cow may have been an exaggeration, it was certainly extraordinary what the men managed to get the guards to bring into the camp. For example, not only could prisoners buy cameras, they could also get the necessary chemicals and dark room equipment to process and print film, as well as spare parts for the various clandestine radios within the camp.

The Red Cross and YMCA supplied books, sports equipment, musical instruments, scripts for plays, gramaphones and records. The library

Kriegsgefangenenlager   Datum: Nov. 13ᵗʰ 1962

Dear Win, Received fourteen letters this week - one from
Doff reporting pastures new - also Selv, Ginge, Dad's, Ruff Win Noth,
Alan Steele and Kit, also Ian Blair and Prof. Hudson. Simply
stupendous! wish I could answer them all. Have lost our
tin-opener - calamitous. So Ginge is helping the Air Force?
great! Weather grows colder - plenty clothes, plenty
blankets, plenty big fire, big eats, whoopee! love Dudley.

A postcard Dudley sent from Stalag 383 to his sister Win.

had over 13 000 books and a big stable was
converted into a school that was open twelve
hours a day and in which sixty different classes
were run every day for its 3500 students.
Amazingly, exam scripts in a huge variety of
subjects were sent to the camp from England, via
Switzerland and then returned to England to be
marked, and eventually the prisoners received
their results. Two theatres put on plays and
musical shows and various orchestras and choirs
played and sang music.

One of the most popular events staged at
the theatre was the light opera, *The Mikado*. The
chorus was made up of Welsh coal miners all
dressed as Japanese women and like the rest of
the cast, they wore costumes made by the men
themselves. A regular visitor to the theatre was
the Commandant and his senior staff. He was so
impressed with *The Mikado* that he stopped roll
call in the camp for three days. Another insight
into his compassion towards the prisoners was
that although Hitler had banned the singing of
the British National Anthem, he allowed it, after
he and his staff discretely left the theatre at the
end of plays. It's easy to imagine the passion

that they sang *God Save the King* from within the
walls of the theatre surrounded by the barbed
wire fence of the camp. He also arranged for the
Berlin Theatre Company to lend the costumes
for *The Merchant of Venice* so the men could put on
the play.

The old saying that the way to a man's heart is
through his stomach could never have been truer
than when that man was a prisoner of war and
he received a Red Cross food parcel. Not only
did the parcels boost morale, they kept hearts
beating by adding calories lacking in the German
rations.

On 13 September 1941, a few months after
arriving at Stalag XVIIID at Marburg, Dudley
wrote to his sister Win about receiving his first
Red Cross food parcels:
*'We have had two of their parcels and two more are on
the way; it is simply wonderful what they have put into
them, what they mean to us is more than I can say.'*

In another letter to Win, also from Marburg
dated 26 Jan 1942, he writes:

A huge amount of time and effort went into the costumes,
makeup and sets for the plays put on at Stalag 383.

Back and front of the Souvenir programme for Christmas 1943 at Stalag 383 with the cover advertising The Mikado *and* Puss in Boots.

'I'd better tell you how the parcels are issued—they are issued three times a week, three mates go shares in the meat foods, one draws on Monday, one Wednesday, and one Friday—the meats are usually 1 large tin fish, 1 large tin bully beef, tin of M & V [meat and vege], tin of meat loaf, with boiled potatoes you can see we have some good meals, we can also buy mustard and beetroot at the Canteen, and beer! I read books in the daytime and when the boys come in from work and the dishes are washed we play bridge till "lights out". We have a weekly newspaper "The Camp" which gives us war news. All these amentities and Europe too, would I give for a seat at your table tonight. My love to Aunts and Uncles all.'

It is no exaggeration to say that these food parcels made the difference between life and death for thousands of prisoners of war and at the end of the war almost 20 million had been delivered to prisoner-of-war camps. But, it was a tenuous lifeline and although each man was supposed to receive a parcel a week, there were often times when the parcels did not get through and it reinforced to everybody just how vulnerable they were.

It is not surprising how often Dudley mentions them in *Alison's Book* and how often his drawings include little parcels with crosses on them. While Red Cross food parcels supplied calories, mail from home was the mental icing on the cake.

On October 25 1941, while at Marburg and six months after his capture in Greece, Dudley wrote in a letter to his sister Kath (Alison's mother): *'Life is lived in moments and I am telling you that one of my greatest and most precious moments was when I received my first mail from New Zealand.'*

In a letter to his sister Dods, written from Stalag 383 on 12 July 1943, Dudley writes about parcels, recycling and gardening: *'I received a very welcome parcel from Win recently, and though its intrinsic value is incalculable to one in my position, my nature is such that I value far more the loving thought which prompted its dispatch. Talking of values , there is absolutely no waste in a parcel — the string may end up as a clothes line or in a broom in lieu of hair, the brown paper we use for covering books, wrapping etc. (lovely little abbreviation etc.) the cloth, for our boiled puddings, the choc. wrappers serve as scribbling papers, the blue cellophane for eye shades, the choc. tins receptacles for tea, sugar etc., and the adhesive tape is most useful mending specs., mounting pictures etc. Our vegetable gardens are yielding plentiful supplies of lettuce and radish, the potatoes, green peas, and beet are not quite ready yet, considering the light soil and lack of manure they make a brave show.'*

While there was no limit to how many letters a prisoner of war could receive, they could only send out four letter-cards (postcards) and two letters a month. The sheer volume of mail in and out of the camp was unimaginable. For example, in one week in November 1943, when the population at Stalag 383 was 4500 men, 8500 letters went out and 5500 came in. While Red Cross parcels and letters kept mind and body together, keeping busy was also important for men who did not know how long they were going to be in captivity.

In a letter to his sister Dods dated 19 March 1943 Dudley writes:
'The weather is glorious: football, hockey, basketball and other sports are in full swing; there are a lot of colds about, heady ones, but that's a minor trouble. My chief indoor pastimes are Bridge and knotty Crosswords, e.g. CLUE: Four in a glass reversed? ANSWER: Snivel. That one stuck me for a whole day. When we run out of tea, coffee and cocoa, we burn bread to a cinder and use ashes in lieu of; it is drinkable, try it! Now that the money is rattling in it's a pity it hasn't more value – still it will keep. I am very fit and hoping a little, now and then, that it won't be long.'

In a letter to his sister Win written on 24 July 1943, Dudley writes about keeping busy:
'After a very wintry spell the weather is now glorious, cricket, basketball, football, swimming, sunbathing and school speed the hours away – in a few weeks we'll have been in this camp a year – gadzooks! but its far too long methinks. Quite a number of the chaps are engaged in crochet-work – necessitating the unraveling of countless old socks, scarves, pullovers, mittens for wool to make bed spreads to keep them warm through the winter, – some are real experts. I haven't started because I'm well off for blankets and I'm still optimistic enough to think

they won't be needed. I haven't finished all my parcel chocolate yet – it's a standby – I'm wearing the braces. I wanted the mirror so's I could preserve my old one which I had turned into a picture frame of Mother and Alison, I hope to bring it home. Our Red Cross parcels arrive regularly and the N.Z. Patriotic Society never miss with their monthly 200 cigarette parcel – for which I am most grateful – and all other services are up to date, so why worry? Don't fail to scatter my love and regards when you visit our Aunts and relations; to tell you the truth my love, I am growing in appreciation of my relatives, near and far.'

Scene from Little Red Riding Hood *at Stalag 383. In the harsh winter of 1944/1945 the wolf wore his costume all the time to keep warm.*

Dudley's remarkable journey of captivity finally ended on May 1 1945 in Straubing, approximately 30 km south of Regensberg and three days march from Stalag 383, when he and thousands of other prisoners were liberated by American forces. After all this Dudley really should have the last word. It comes from a letter he wrote to his sister Win, my grandmother, on the 13 September 1941, almost a year before he started *Alison's Book*. He started the letter with, *'Some day the story will be told. I don't think it worth while starting it in a letter.'* Thank you for your story Dudley.

Acknowledgements

I would like to thank all of Dudley's family and friends who have contributed letters and anecdotes to help take me back to a time I wasn't around to witness. Thanks to Dudley's nephew's Bill Ogston and his wife Doreen, and Geoff Hamilton and his wife Wendy for sharing Dudley's surviving letters and photographs. Thanks also to his niece Pauline Cameron for sharing postcards and photographs. Thanks to Dudley's nephew Jim Pollard, my uncle, for letters, suggestions of relatives to contact and memories of being a child in New Zealand during WWII. Thanks to my father and Dudley's nephew, David Pollard for his wonderful memories of Dudley and his mother Win as she lived through Dudley's capture, captivity and return. Thanks to Ian Collins at Lincoln University for helping to bring Dudley to life during the time he was librarian before and after WWII. A special thank you to Terry Hitchings for his military knowledge and his insightful humanity on what it must have been like to be captured and become a prisoner of war. Thanks also to Terry's brother, retired Brigadier Geof Hitchings for transcribing Dudley's military records. Thanks to curators Jo Condon and Sarah Whitehead at Canterbury Museum and Kimberly Connor at the University of San Francisco for their helpful comments on the introduction. Thanks to Canterbury Museum for permission to reproduce the diary (ARC 1992.36). And of course, a special thank you to Alison, for sharing her memories and for being a niece who was three years old when Dudley left for war, but nevertheless inspired him to write *Alison's Book* for her.

Finally, I must thank my wife Cynthia for breathing life into my writing and for putting up with me having one foot in Stalag 383 for the last eighteen months.

Dudley in late 1940.

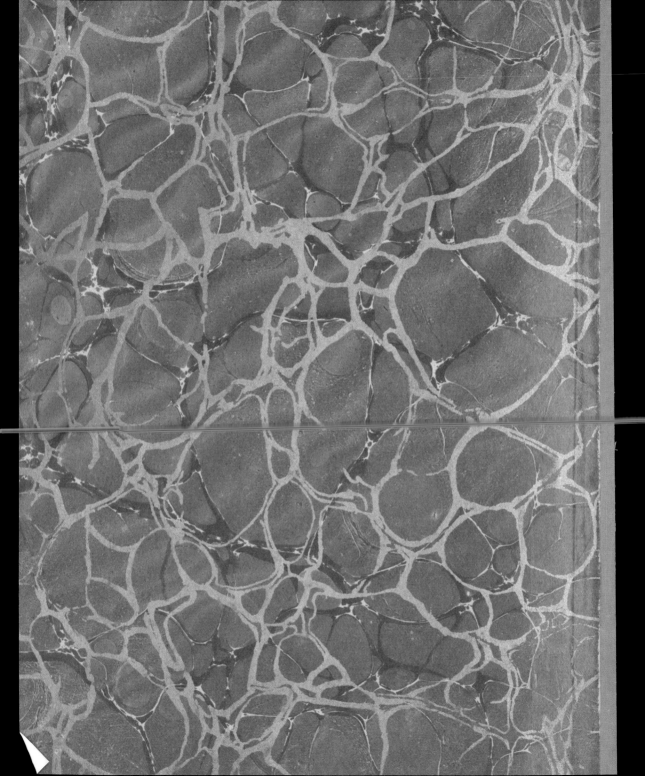